YOSEMITE NATIONAL PARK
TRAVEL GUIDE 2025

The Complete Manual to Exploring Majestic Landscapes and Outdoor Adventures

Dexter Tillery

Table of Contents

INTRODUCTION

Why Visit Yosemite?

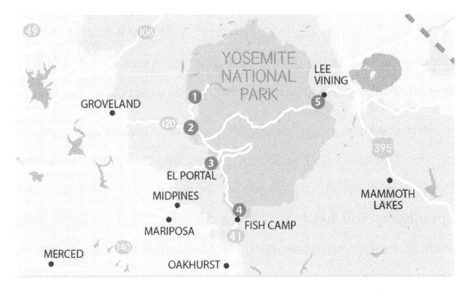

Yosemite National Park is a place of stunning beauty, where nature's wonders are on full display. Picture yourself surrounded by towering granite cliffs, giant sequoia trees, and breathtaking waterfalls. Yosemite is famous for its incredible landscapes, including world-renowned sites like El Capitan, Half Dome, and Yosemite Falls. Whether you're a nature lover, an adventurer, or just someone looking to relax, Yosemite has something to offer for everyone. It's a destination that will leave you in awe, no matter how many times you visit.

What makes Yosemite truly special is its variety of landscapes. The park has deep valleys, wide meadows, forests filled with giant sequoia trees, and some of the tallest waterfalls in North America. Imagine standing at the base of Yosemite Falls, with mist spraying your face as water crashes down from over 2,400 feet above. Or picture yourself hiking through the quiet Mariposa Grove, home to trees that have been growing for thousands of years.

No matter where you go in the park, you'll be surrounded by natural beauty. The cliffs and rock formations, like El Capitan and Half Dome, are especially famous among rock climbers and adventurers. You don't have to be a climber, though, to appreciate their grandeur. Just looking up at these massive formations is enough to leave you speechless.

Yosemite's landscapes change with the seasons, too. In spring, the waterfalls are at their fullest, roaring with snowmelt. In the summer, wildflowers bloom in the meadows. Autumn brings golden hues as the trees change color, and winter covers the park in a blanket of snow, making it a peaceful wonderland. This constant change makes Yosemite a park that never looks the same twice.

Why Yosemite is a Must-Visit Destination

Yosemite is not just about seeing beautiful places—it's about feeling connected to nature. There is something about the vastness of the park that makes you feel small but in a good way. You can stand in the valley and gaze up at cliffs that tower thousands of feet above you. It is humbling and awe-inspiring, reminding you of the power and beauty of the natural world.

One of the best things about Yosemite is that it offers something for everyone. If you are an adventurer, there are endless opportunities for hiking, rock climbing, and exploring. If you prefer a slower pace, you can take a leisurely walk through the meadows, sit by the Merced River, or enjoy a scenic drive through the park. Yosemite is also a great destination for families, with lot of kid-friendly trails and activities.

How to Use This Guide

This guide is designed to help you get the most out of your visit to Yosemite. Whether you're a day-tripper, a hiker, or someone who simply loves nature, this guide will provide you with all the information you need to plan your trip and explore the park. It is like having a local expert with you, showing you the best places to go and giving you tips on how to make your trip easier and more enjoyable.

Who Is This Guide For?

This guide is for everyone, whether you're visiting Yosemite for the first time, or you've been here before. Here's how it can help you:

Day-Trippers: If you're only spending a day in the park, this guide will show you how to make the most of your time. We'll highlight the must-see spots and give you tips on how to fit them all into a single day. Even if you only have a few hours, there's plenty you can see and do in Yosemite.

Hikers: Yosemite is famous for its hiking trails, and this guide will help you choose the right ones for your skill level.

Nature Enthusiasts: If you are visiting Yosemite to enjoy its wildlife and natural wonders, we have got you covered. This guide will point you to the best spots for birdwatching, wildlife viewing, and nature photography.

Tips for Navigating the Guide

This guide is organized in a way that makes it easy to find what you're looking for.

Planning Your Trip: Start with the sections that help you plan your visit, including tips on the best time to visit the park. Yosemite is beautiful year-round, but each season offers a unique experience.

Exploring the Park: Once you have planned your trip, use the guide to learn about Yosemite's most famous landmarks. We will provide maps and directions to help you find the park's top attractions, including Yosemite Valley, Glacier Point, and the Mariposa Grove of giant sequoias.

Hiking and Adventure: If you are planning to hike, head to the hiking section of the guide. Each trail is described in detail, with information on difficulty, length, and what you will see along the way. We also include tips on what to pack, how to stay safe, and how to get the most out of your hiking experience.

Wildlife and Nature Watching: For those interested in seeing Yosemite's wildlife, this guide will show you the best places to go. We will tell you where to look for bears, deer, and other animals, as well as tips on how to observe them safely and respectfully.

Packing and Preparing: Do not forget to check out our packing tips. Yosemite is a wild place, and it is important to come prepared.

CHAPTER 1

PLANNING YOUR YOSEMITE ADVENTURE

P lanning a trip to Yosemite is an exciting part of the journey. The park offers something special throughout the year, but choosing the right time to visit depends on what you're looking for.

Best Time to Visit

There's no wrong time to visit Yosemite, but each season brings its own advantages and challenges. Knowing what to expect will help you plan your visit and make the most of your time in this incredible national park.

Season-by-Season Breakdown: Pros & Cons

Spring (March to May)

Spring is one of the most popular times to visit Yosemite, and for good reason. As the snow from winter begins to melt, the waterfalls flow at their peak, creating a dramatic and awe-inspiring display. The meadows are lush and green, and wildflowers begin to bloom, adding splashes of color to the landscape. It's also a great time for wildlife viewing, as many animals become more active after the long winter months.

Pros:

- Waterfalls are at their fullest.

- Wildflowers bloom in the meadows.

- Mild temperatures make hiking enjoyable.

- Less crowded than summer.

Cons:

- Some high-elevation trails and roads may still be closed due to snow.

- Weather can be unpredictable, with occasional rain or snow.

Summer (June to August)

Summer is the busiest time of year in Yosemite. The weather is warm and sunny, making it ideal for hiking, camping, and exploring the park's higher elevations. All the roads and trails are open, including the famous Tioga Road and Glacier Point Road. However, with the good weather comes large crowds, especially in popular areas like Yosemite Valley and Glacier Point.

Pros:

- Warm, sunny weather perfect for outdoor activities.

- All roads and trails are open.

- Access to high-elevation areas like Tuolumne Meadows.

Cons:

- The park is crowded, especially in Yosemite Valley.
- Waterfalls may dry up by late summer.
- Lodging and campsites are harder to book and more expensive.

Fall (September to November)

Fall in Yosemite is a time of quiet beauty. The summer crowds have mostly gone, leaving the park peaceful and serene. The leaves begin to change color, especially in late September and October, turning the valley into a golden wonderland. The cooler temperatures make hiking more comfortable, and while the waterfalls may not be as impressive as in spring, the crisp air and stunning scenery make it a fantastic time to visit.

Pros:

- Fewer crowds and more peaceful atmosphere.
- Beautiful autumn colors in the trees and meadows.
- Cooler temperatures are great for hiking.
- Easier to find lodging and campsites.

Cons:

- Waterfalls are at their lowest or may dry up completely.
- Days are shorter, and nights can be chilly.

- Some facilities and roads may close toward the end of fall.

Winter transforms Yosemite into a magical, snowy landscape. While many parts of the park are closed due to snow, Yosemite Valley remains open year-round, and it's a great time to experience the park without the crowds. Winter sports enthusiasts will enjoy skiing, snowshoeing, and ice skating at Badger Pass Ski Area. The snow-covered granite cliffs and frozen waterfalls offer a peaceful, almost otherworldly beauty.

Pros:

- Yosemite is much less crowded in winter.
- Snow-covered landscapes are stunning and serene.
- Great for winter sports like skiing and snowshoeing.
- Lodging prices are generally lower.

Cons:

- Some roads and trails, including Tioga Road and Glacier Point Road, are closed due to snow.
- Cold temperatures and shorter days.
- Limited access to certain parts of the park.

Popular Events and Festivals

While Yosemite is always a wonderful destination, certain events and festivals add extra excitement to your visit. These events celebrate the natural beauty, history, and culture of the park, offering unique opportunities to connect with Yosemite in a deeper way.

Yosemite Earth Day Festival (April)

Every April, Yosemite celebrates Earth Day with a series of events focused on sustainability, environmental awareness, and conservation. The festival includes educational exhibits, volunteer activities, and family-friendly events like ranger-led walks and talks. It's a great time to visit if you're interested in learning more about how Yosemite works to protect its natural environment.

Yosemite Facelift (September)

Yosemite Facelift is an annual volunteer event aimed at cleaning up the park after the busy summer season. Thousands of volunteers from all over the country come together to help remove trash and restore the park's beauty. It's a rewarding way to give back to the park while meeting like-minded people who care about preserving Yosemite for future generations.

Chef's Holidays (January)

In the heart of winter, Yosemite hosts Chef's Holidays, a series of events celebrating gourmet food and wine. Some of the top chefs from across the country gather at The Ahwahnee Hotel to share their culinary expertise through cooking demonstrations, tastings, and multi-course meals. If you're a foodie, this is a unique way to experience Yosemite's charm combined with world-class dining.

Yosemite Renaissance Art Exhibit (February to May)

The Yosemite Renaissance Art Exhibit showcases artwork inspired by Yosemite and the Sierra Nevada. Held annually, the exhibit features paintings, sculptures, photography, and mixed media, highlighting the connection between art and nature. It's a beautiful way to experience the park through the eyes of talented artists.

Full Moon Snowshoe Walks (Winter)

During winter, Yosemite offers guided full moon snowshoe walks, where you can explore the snowy landscape by the light of the moon. These ranger-led walks are a peaceful and magical way to experience the quiet, snow-covered wilderness. The glow of the moon on the snow creates an unforgettable atmosphere.

Starry Skies Over Yosemite (Year-Round)

Yosemite offers some of the best stargazing opportunities in California, thanks to its remote location and minimal light pollution. Throughout the year, the park hosts stargazing programs, where rangers and astronomers guide you through the night sky, pointing out constellations, planets, and distant galaxies. Whether you're visiting in summer or winter, a night under the stars in Yosemite is an awe-inspiring experience.

Getting to Yosemite

Reaching Yosemite National Park can be a scenic journey, whether you're traveling by car, plane, or train. Nestled in the Sierra Nevada mountains of California, Yosemite is accessible from several major cities and offers various transportation options depending on your location and preferences. Once you've arrived, getting around the park is easy thanks to well-maintained roads, shuttle services, and plenty of opportunities to explore on foot.

Closest Airports, Train Stations, and Driving Routes

Airports

If you're flying to Yosemite, the nearest airports offer convenient access to the park, but keep in mind that you'll still need to drive or take a shuttle from the airport to the park entrance.

Fresno Yosemite International Airport (FAT)

Distance to Yosemite: Approximately 65 miles (1.5 to 2 hours drive)

Fresno Yosemite International is the closest major airport to the park, located about 1.5 hours from the southern entrance (via Highway 41). Many major airlines fly into Fresno, making it a convenient option if you plan to rent a car or take a shuttle service to the park.

Sacramento International Airport (SMF)

Distance to Yosemite: Approximately 170 miles (3.5 to 4 hours drive)

Sacramento International Airport offers more flight options and is located about 3.5 to 4 hours from Yosemite. This is a good option if you're combining a trip to California's capital city or northern regions with your Yosemite adventure.

San Francisco International Airport (SFO)

Distance to Yosemite: Approximately 200 miles (4 to 4.5 hours drive)

San Francisco International is one of the busiest airports on the West Coast and offers numerous domestic and international flight options. From San Francisco, it's about a 4 to 4.5-hour drive to

Yosemite. This route is popular if you're planning to spend some time in San Francisco before heading to the park.

Oakland International Airport (OAK)

Distance to Yosemite: Approximately 180 miles (3.5 to 4 hours drive)

Similar to San Francisco International, Oakland International offers a wide range of flights and is slightly closer to Yosemite. It's about a 3.5 to 4-hour drive from Oakland to the park, making it another convenient option for travelers coming from the Bay Area.

Train Stations

If you prefer to take a train, Amtrak provides service to several stations near Yosemite. You'll need to transfer to a bus or shuttle service to reach the park, but this can be a relaxing and scenic way to travel.

Amtrak to Merced Station

The most convenient Amtrak station for Yosemite is in Merced, about 80 miles from the park. From Merced, you can take the YARTS (Yosemite Area Regional Transportation System) bus directly into Yosemite Valley.

Amtrak to Fresno Station

Another option is to take Amtrak to Fresno, where you can either rent a car or catch a YARTS bus to Yosemite. The train ride to Fresno offers beautiful views of California's central valley.

Driving Routes

Driving to Yosemite is a popular choice, especially for those who want the freedom to explore the surrounding areas or visit multiple points of interest within the park. Here are the main routes to Yosemite:

Highway 41 (Southern Route)

This route takes you through Fresno and Oakhurst and leads directly to the park's southern entrance, which is close to the Mariposa Grove of giant sequoias. This is the best route if you're coming from southern California or Fresno.

Highway 120 (Western Route)

Highway 120 is the most direct route from the San Francisco Bay Area and passes through the town of Groveland. It brings you into the park from the west, providing easy access to Yosemite Valley. This route is also known as the Big Oak Flat Entrance.

Highway 140 (Central Route)

Known as the "All-Weather Highway," Highway 140 is often the best option during the winter months, as it's less likely to be affected by snow and ice. It brings you through the town of Mariposa and into Yosemite Valley via the Arch Rock Entrance.

Highway 395 and Tioga Pass (Eastern Route)

If you're coming from the eastern Sierra or Nevada, Highway 395 connects to Yosemite via Tioga Pass (Highway 120 East). This scenic route takes you through the high country, offering spectacular views, but Tioga Pass is closed in winter due to snow, typically from November to May.

Transportation Options Within the Park

Once you've arrived in Yosemite, navigating the park is easy thanks to a variety of transportation options. Whether you prefer to drive, take a shuttle, or explore on foot, there are several ways to get around the park and see its famous landmarks.

Driving in Yosemite

If you are driving your own vehicle or a rental car, you'll have the flexibility to explore Yosemite at your own pace. The park's roads are well-maintained, but they can become crowded during peak season (summer) and on weekends. Parking is available at key locations, such as Yosemite Valley, Glacier Point, and Mariposa Grove, but it can fill up quickly, especially in the middle of the day. To avoid traffic and parking issues, it's best to arrive early or visit during off-peak times.

Shuttle Services

Yosemite offers a free shuttle service within the most popular areas of the park, making it easy to get around without needing a car. The shuttles are eco-friendly and help reduce traffic congestion, especially in Yosemite Valley.

Yosemite Valley Shuttle

The Yosemite Valley Shuttle operates year-round and makes stops at all major points of interest within Yosemite Valley, including Yosemite Falls, El Capitan, Half Dome Village, and the Visitor Center. The shuttle runs every 10 to 20 minutes, and it's a convenient way to explore the valley without worrying about parking.

Glacier Point Shuttle

In the summer months, a shuttle runs from Badger Pass to Glacier Point, one of the park's most scenic overlooks. This is a great option if you want to take in the views from Glacier Point without the hassle of driving the winding road yourself.

Mariposa Grove Shuttle

The Mariposa Grove of Giant Sequoias is a must-see, and during peak seasons, the Mariposa Grove Shuttle runs from the parking area at the South Entrance to the grove itself. This service helps protect the sensitive environment of the grove and reduces vehicle traffic in this special area.

YARTS (Yosemite Area Regional Transportation System)

For those staying outside the park or traveling without a car, YARTS provides convenient bus service to Yosemite from surrounding areas. YARTS buses run from locations like Merced, Fresno, and Mammoth Lakes, and they drop passengers off at key locations within Yosemite Valley. YARTS is a great option if you want to avoid the hassle of parking and driving within the park.

Biking

Biking is a fun and eco-friendly way to explore Yosemite, especially in Yosemite Valley. The park has over 12 miles of paved bike paths that take you to major attractions, including Yosemite Falls, Mirror Lake, and El Capitan Meadow. You can bring your own bike or rent one from several locations within the valley. Biking is a great way to avoid the crowds and experience the park at a leisurely pace.

Walking and Hiking

Yosemite is a park made for exploring on foot. Many of the key sights are easily accessible via short walks or hikes, and the park offers trails for all skill levels. Whether you're taking a stroll to Lower Yosemite Falls or embarking on a challenging hike up to Half Dome, walking and hiking are some of the best ways to experience Yosemite's natural beauty up close.

Tour Buses

If you prefer a guided experience, Yosemite offers several bus tours that provide narrated journeys through the park's most famous landmarks. The Yosemite Valley Floor Tour, for example, is a two-hour guided tour that takes you to iconic spots like El Capitan, Bridalveil Fall, and Tunnel View. These tours are a great option for visitors who want to learn more about the park's history and natural features while enjoying a relaxing ride.

Where to Stay

Yosemite National Park offers a wide range of accommodations, from rustic campsites and cabins to luxury hotels, ensuring there's something to suit every traveler's needs and preferences. Whether you want to stay close to the park's main attractions or prefer a quieter spot outside the park, choosing the right place to stay can enhance your Yosemite experience. This section will help you understand your options and make the best choice for your visit.

Hotels, Cabins, and Campsites: Choosing the Right Accommodation

Hotels

If you're looking for comfort and convenience, Yosemite's hotels provide an excellent option. Staying in a hotel inside or near the park allows you to enjoy modern amenities like comfortable beds, Wi-Fi, and on-site dining, making your stay more relaxing after a long day of exploring.

The Ahwahnee Hotel (Inside the Park)

One of the most famous hotels in Yosemite, The Ahwahnee offers luxurious accommodations with stunning views of Yosemite Valley. Known for its grand architecture and historic charm, this four-star hotel offers well-appointed rooms, suites, and cottages. The Ahwahnee also features fine dining, an outdoor pool, and easy access to key attractions like Yosemite Falls and Half Dome.

Yosemite Valley Lodge (Inside the Park)

Located near Yosemite Falls, this family-friendly lodge is perfect for travelers who want to stay close to the action. The rooms are comfortable and simple, offering great views and proximity to Yosemite Valley's main attractions. Yosemite Valley Lodge also has an on-site restaurant, bike rentals, and easy access to shuttle stops.

Wawona Hotel (Inside the Park)

For a more peaceful, historic experience, consider staying at the Wawona Hotel. Situated near the park's southern entrance, this charming hotel offers Victorian-style rooms with no TVs, allowing guests to fully immerse themselves in the tranquility of Yosemite. The Wawona Hotel is close to the Mariposa Grove of Giant Sequoias and is a great base for those looking to explore the park's quieter areas.

Rush Creek Lodge (Outside the Park)

Located just outside the park's western entrance, Rush Creek Lodge is a modern, family-friendly resort offering a range of accommodations, from lodge rooms to cabins. With amenities like a heated pool, a spa, and on-site dining, it's a great choice for those looking for a balance of comfort and outdoor adventure.

Cabins

For a more rustic experience that still offers comfort, Yosemite's cabins provide a great middle ground between camping and staying in a hotel. Cabins are ideal for families, groups, or those who want a little more privacy and a connection with nature.

Curry Village (Inside the Park)

Curry Village, also known as Half Dome Village, offers a variety of cabins, including heated and unheated tent cabins, wood-sided cabins with private bathrooms, and more. This popular spot is in Yosemite Valley and provides easy access to many of the park's top attractions. Curry Village is a great option if you want a cabin experience with easy access to dining options and a bustling atmosphere.

Housekeeping Camp (Inside the Park)

If you want to be even closer to nature, Housekeeping Camp offers open-air cabins right by the Merced River. These units have three walls and a roof, allowing you to sleep under the stars while still having access to beds and a fire ring for cooking. It's a great option for those who want a camping experience without the hassle of setting up a tent.

Campsites

For outdoor enthusiasts, camping in Yosemite is one of the best ways to experience the park's natural beauty. Yosemite offers several campgrounds with various amenities, from basic tent sites to more developed campgrounds with showers and RV hookups.

Upper Pines Campground (Inside the Park)

One of the most popular campgrounds in Yosemite, Upper Pines is located in Yosemite Valley and is open year-round. It offers 238 sites for tents and RVs and is close to many of the park's most famous sights. This campground provides a true Yosemite experience, with towering trees and stunning views of the surrounding cliffs.

Tuolumne Meadows Campground (Inside the Park)

If you want to escape the crowds in Yosemite Valley, Tuolumne Meadows Campground offers a more peaceful, high-country camping experience. Located along the Tioga Road, this large campground is open during the summer months and provides access to some of Yosemite's best hiking trails and scenic spots, including the Tuolumne River and Soda Springs.

Bridalveil Creek Campground (Inside the Park)

Another great option for summer camping, Bridalveil Creek Campground is located on Glacier Point Road, offering access to the park's high country. This campground is a bit more remote, making it perfect for visitors looking for a quieter, less crowded experience.

Campgrounds Outside the Park

If you're unable to secure a campsite inside the park, there are plenty of campgrounds located just outside Yosemite's entrances. These campgrounds, such as Hodgdon Meadow and Crane Flat, provide easy access to the park and often have more availability, especially during the busy summer season.

Lodging Inside vs. Outside the Park

Choosing whether to stay inside or outside Yosemite depends on your budget, personal preferences, and the type of experience you're looking for. Both options have their advantages and disadvantages, and this section will help you decide which is best for your trip.

Lodging Inside the Park

Staying inside the park offers several key benefits, including easy access to Yosemite's major attractions and the convenience of being close to everything you want to see and do. If you're staying in Yosemite Valley, you'll be able to walk or take a short shuttle ride to landmarks like Yosemite Falls, El Capitan, and Half Dome. This can save you time, especially if you're visiting during peak seasons when traffic can be heavy.

Advantages:

- You're close to all the main sights, making it easy to explore the park without long drives.
- Staying in the park allows you to fully experience Yosemite's natural beauty, whether it's watching the sunrise from your cabin or hearing the sounds of wildlife at night.
- You won't need to worry about commuting into the park each day, which is especially important during busy summer months when parking can be limited.

Disadvantages:

- Accommodations inside the park tend to be more expensive, especially during peak season. Booking well in advance is essential to secure a spot.
- Lodging inside the park fills up quickly, so you'll need to plan ahead. Reservations for hotels, cabins, and campsites can be made up to a year in advance and often sell out early.

Lodging Outside the Park

If you're unable to find accommodation inside the park or prefer more affordable options, staying outside Yosemite can be a great alternative. Many towns near the park's entrances, such as Mariposa, Oakhurst, and Groveland, offer a range of hotels, motels, and vacation rentals. While you'll need to drive into the park each day, staying outside gives you access to more budget-friendly accommodations and a wider variety of restaurants and amenities.

Advantages:

- More Affordable: Lodging outside the park tends to be less expensive, and you'll have a wider range of options to choose from, including chain hotels, motels, and vacation rentals.
- More Dining and Amenities: Towns near the park often have more dining options, grocery stores, and other amenities, making it easier to stock up on supplies for your trip.
- Flexibility: If you're visiting other nearby attractions, such as the Sierra National Forest or Bass Lake, staying outside the park can give you more flexibility to explore the surrounding area.

Disadvantages:

- Longer Commute: Depending on where you stay, it can take 30 minutes to over an hour to drive into Yosemite Valley.
- Limited Park Experience: Staying outside the park means you will not be as immersed in Yosemite's natural surroundings, and you may miss early morning or late evening activities like stargazing or sunrise hikes.

Chapter 2

ESSENTIAL PACKING AND PREPARATION

Packing for your Yosemite adventure is an important step to ensure a safe, comfortable, and enjoyable trip. The weather and conditions in Yosemite can vary greatly depending on the time of year, so being prepared with the right gear is crucial. This chapter will guide you through what to pack for each season, helping you to be ready for all the adventures Yosemite has to offer.

What to Pack for Each Season

Each season in Yosemite comes with its own set of conditions, from hot summer days to chilly winter nights. Knowing what to pack will not only make your trip more comfortable but will also help you stay safe in Yosemite's rugged environment.

Summer Essentials: Sun Protection and Lightweight Gear

Summer in Yosemite (June to August) can be warm to hot, especially in Yosemite Valley, where temperatures often reach 80°F to 90°F (27°C to 32°C). However, higher elevations like Glacier Point and Tuolumne Meadows are cooler, so you'll need to pack accordingly. Summer is also the peak hiking season, so lightweight gear and sun protection are key.

When it comes to clothing, aim for light, breathable, and moisture-wicking materials that will keep you cool and comfortable in the heat.

- Lightweight, breathable clothing: Pack short-sleeve shirts, lightweight pants or shorts, and moisture-wicking fabrics like polyester or merino wool to stay cool while hiking.

- Hat and sunglasses: A wide-brimmed hat will provide extra protection from the sun, and sunglasses with UV protection are a must to shield your eyes from the bright sunlight.

- Layers: Even in summer, temperatures can drop in the early mornings and evenings, especially in higher elevations. Bring a light jacket or fleece for these cooler times.

- Comfortable hiking shoes: If you plan to hike, sturdy, broken-in hiking boots or shoes with good grip and support are essential. Consider shoes that are breathable to keep your feet cool during long hikes.

Sun Protection

The sun is intense in Yosemite, particularly at higher elevations, so protecting yourself from sunburn and dehydration is crucial.

- Sunscreen: Use a high-SPF sunscreen (at least SPF 30) and reapply throughout the day, especially when hiking.
- Lip balm with SPF: Don't forget to protect your lips from the sun's rays.
- Reusable water bottle or hydration pack: Staying hydrated is key, especially when hiking in the summer heat. Bring a refillable water bottle or a hydration bladder that fits into your backpack.
- Insect repellent: Mosquitoes and other insects can be common, especially near water, so pack insect repellent to avoid bites.

Hiking and Camping Gear

If you plan to explore Yosemite's trails or camp overnight, you'll need some essential gear.

- *Daypack:* A small, lightweight backpack for day hikes to carry water, snacks, sunscreen, and other essentials.
- *Map and compass or GPS device:* Yosemite has many trails, and cell service is limited, so having a physical map or GPS device will help you stay on track.
- *First aid kit:* A basic first aid kit with band-aids, antiseptic wipes, blister treatment, and pain relievers is a good idea for any outdoor adventure.

- *Portable charger:* If you plan to take photos or use your phone for navigation, a portable charger can keep your devices powered throughout the day.
- *Lightweight camping gear:* If you are camping, make sure you bring a lightweight tent, sleeping bag (rated for summer temperatures), and a sleeping pad for comfort.

Winter Must-Haves: Warm Clothing and Snow Gear

Winter in Yosemite (December to February) is a completely different experience, as the park is often blanketed in snow, especially at higher elevations. Yosemite Valley remains accessible, but temperatures can drop below freezing, and snow gear is necessary for those planning to explore. Whether you're enjoying a winter hike, skiing at Badger Pass, or just soaking in the snow-covered landscapes, staying warm and dry is essential.

Clothing

Layering is key for winter in Yosemite. You'll want to stay warm, but it's important to be able to adjust your clothing as you warm up during physical activities like hiking or snowshoeing.

- *Base layer:* Start with a moisture-wicking base layer made of materials like merino wool or synthetic fabrics. Avoid cotton, as it retains moisture and can make you cold.

- *Insulating layer:* A fleece jacket or down sweater will provide warmth while still being lightweight.

- *Outer layer:* A waterproof and windproof jacket is essential to protect you from snow, rain, and wind. Choose a jacket with insulation if you're prone to getting cold.

- *Warm pants:* For outdoor activities, opt for insulated, waterproof pants or snow pants. If you're hiking, thermal leggings under your regular hiking pants can keep you warm.

- *Hat and gloves:* A warm beanie and insulated gloves are necessary for protecting your head and hands from the cold. If you're using your phone or camera, consider touchscreen-compatible gloves.

- *Wool socks and sturdy boots:* Wool socks will keep your feet warm even if they get wet, and waterproof boots with good traction are a must for navigating snowy or icy terrain.

Snow Gear

If you're planning to spend time in the snow, whether skiing, snowshoeing, or just hiking in winter conditions, specialized gear will help keep you safe and comfortable.

- *Microspikes or crampons:* Winter trails can be icy, so bringing microspikes or crampons that attach to your boots will give you better traction on slippery surfaces.
- *Snowshoes:* If you plan to explore deeper snow, snowshoes can help you hike through areas that would otherwise be difficult to traverse. Many places in Yosemite rent snowshoes if you don't have your own.
- *Gaiters:* These can help keep snow out of your boots when walking through deeper snow.

Winter Accessories

These additional items will make your winter trip more enjoyable by ensuring you stay warm and comfortable in the snowy conditions.

Neck gaiter or scarf: Protect your neck and face from cold winds and snow.

Hand warmers: Disposable hand warmers can be slipped into your gloves or pockets to provide extra warmth on cold days.

Ski goggles or sunglasses: Snow reflects sunlight, making it very bright. Sunglasses or ski goggles with UV protection will shield your eyes from the glare.

Winter Camping and Overnight Gear

If you're planning to camp in the winter, extra preparation is needed to stay safe and warm overnight.

Four-season tent: A tent designed for winter camping is necessary to withstand cold temperatures and snow.

Cold weather sleeping bag: Look for a sleeping bag rated for temperatures below freezing to ensure you stay warm overnight.

Sleeping pad: An insulated sleeping pad will keep you off the cold ground and add an extra layer of warmth.

Permits and Reservations

Yosemite is a popular destination, and certain areas of the park require permits and reservations to manage the number of visitors and protect the environment. Whether you're entering the park for a day trip or planning to hike iconic trails, it's important to understand the permit process to ensure your trip goes smoothly.

Entry Fees, Passes, and Wilderness Permits

Entry Fees and Passes

Yosemite National Park requires an entry fee, which can be paid at the park entrance or online in advance. The fee covers access to the park for seven consecutive days. Here are the options:

Private vehicle: $35 per vehicle, valid for seven days.

Motorcycle: $30 per motorcycle, valid for seven days.

Individual (on foot, bicycle, or horseback): $20 per person, valid for seven days.

If you are planning to visit multiple national parks within a year, consider purchasing the **America the Beautiful Pass** for $80. This annual pass grants access to all national parks and federal lands in the U.S.

https://www.nps.gov/anti/planyourvisit/america-the-beautiful-pass-series

Wilderness Permits

If you're planning to camp overnight in Yosemite's backcountry, you'll need a wilderness permit. These permits are required year-round for all overnight stays in the wilderness areas of the park. Wilderness permits are limited to protect the environment and provide a more peaceful experience for visitors.

How to Apply: You can apply for wilderness permits online through Yosemite's website. Reservations open five months in advance, and permits are highly competitive, especially for popular trails.

Walk-Up Permits: A limited number of walk-up permits are available on a first-come, first-served basis at wilderness centers in the park. Arrive early to increase your chances of securing one.

How to Secure Permits for Iconic Trails (Half Dome, etc.)

Some of Yosemite's most famous hikes, like the Half Dome Trail, require special permits due to their popularity and difficulty. Securing a permit can be competitive, so it's important to plan.

Half Dome Permits

The hike to Half Dome is one of the most iconic and challenging hikes in Yosemite. Due to the large number of hikers attempting the trail each year, permits are required for the final ascent, which involves climbing the cables to the summit.

Lottery System: Permits for Half Dome are issued through a lottery system. The preseason lottery opens in March each year, and you can apply for permits for any date during the hiking season (typically late May through mid-October, depending on weather conditions).

Daily Lottery: If you don't secure a permit in the preseason lottery, there's also a daily lottery for a limited number of permits, which opens two days in advance of the desired hiking date.

Fees: There is a non-refundable fee of $10 to enter the lottery. If you are awarded a permit, an additional $10 per person is required to secure the permit.

John Muir Trail (JMT) Permits

If you're planning to hike the John Muir Trail, which runs through Yosemite and beyond, you'll need a wilderness permit. Permits for the JMT are also issued through a lottery system, and demand is high. You can apply for a permit starting 24 weeks in advance of your hike.

Clouds Rest Permits

While the trail to Clouds Rest does not require a permit for day hikers, those planning to camp overnight along the route will need a wilderness permit.

Other Wilderness Trails

For other popular trails and wilderness areas, such as the Yosemite Falls Trail or the Mist Trail leading to Vernal and Nevada Falls, permits are not required for day hikes. However, you will need a wilderness permit if you plan to camp overnight in these areas.

Chapter 3

EXPLORING YOSEMITE'S ICONIC SIGHTS

Yosemite National Park is famous for its stunning landscapes and awe-inspiring natural landmarks. From towering granite cliffs to roaring waterfalls, there is no shortage of breathtaking sights to explore.

Top Must-See Landmarks

El Capitan: The Giant of Granite

Image from Daniel Salcius on Unsplash

Standing at an impressive 3,000 feet (900 meters) above the Yosemite Valley floor, **El Capitan** is one of the most iconic granite formations in the world. Known for its sheer vertical face, El Capitan attracts rock climbers from around the globe who attempt to scale its challenging cliffs. Even if you're not a climber, gazing up at El Capitan from the valley floor is a humbling and awe-inspiring experience.

Best Viewing Spot: One of the best places to view El Capitan is from **El Capitan Meadow,** located along Northside Drive. This spot offers a clear view of the massive rock face, allowing you to fully appreciate its scale and majesty. If you're lucky, you might even spot climbers making their way up the face.

Fun Fact: El Capitan gained worldwide attention in 2017 when climber Alex Honnold completed the first free solo ascent of the cliff, meaning he climbed it without ropes or safety gear. This incredible feat was documented in the award-winning film Free Solo.

Half Dome is perhaps the most recognizable symbol of Yosemite National Park. Its unique shape, resembling a giant dome cut in half, rises nearly 5,000 feet (1,524 meters) above Yosemite Valley. Hiking to the summit of Half Dome is a bucket-list adventure for many visitors, offering panoramic views of the surrounding peaks and valleys.

The Hike: The hike to the top of Half Dome is a challenging 14–16-mile (22-26 km) round trip, typically taking 10-12 hours to complete. The final ascent involves climbing steel cables anchored to the rock face, making it one of the most thrilling hikes in the park. A permit is required to hike to the summit, and it's best suited for experienced hikers.

Best Viewing Spot: For those not hiking, you can still get a splendid view of Half Dome from **Glacier Point** or **Tunnel View**. The shape of the dome is especially striking at sunrise or sunset when the light highlights its dramatic features.

pg. 41

Yosemite Falls: The Tallest Waterfall in North America

Yosemite Falls is one of the park's most iconic features and a must-see for any visitor. Cascading down from the heights of the Sierra Nevada, Yosemite Falls stands at a towering 2,425 feet (739 meters), making it the tallest waterfall in North America. It's actually made up of three sections: Upper Yosemite Fall, the Middle Cascades, and Lower Yosemite Fall, all of which combine to create an impressive and powerful spectacle, especially in spring when the water flow is at its peak.

Best Viewing Spot: The Lower Yosemite Fall Trail offers an easy, family-friendly walk that brings you up close to the base of the falls. For a more comprehensive view of the entire waterfall, head to **Yosemite Village** or **Swinging Bridge**. You can also hike to the top of Yosemite Falls via a strenuous 7.2-mile (11.6 km) round trip trail, which rewards you with a spectacular view of the valley below.

Best Time to Visit: Yosemite Falls is most impressive in late spring and early summer when the snowmelt fuels the flow. By late summer, the waterfall can dry up, so plan your visit accordingly.

Scenic Drives and Vistas

Glacier Point: The Best View of Yosemite Valley

Perched at an elevation of 7,214 feet (2,199 meters), **Glacier Point** offers what many consider the best view of Yosemite Valley, with stunning vistas of Half Dome, Yosemite Falls, and the high country beyond. The view from Glacier Point provides a sweeping panorama that lets you take in the vast beauty of Yosemite in one glance.

Driving Route: Glacier Point is accessible via a 16-mile (26 km) scenic drive from Yosemite Valley. The drive itself is full of incredible views, and there are several pullouts along the way where you can stop and admire the scenery. The road to Glacier Point is typically open from late May to October, depending on snow conditions.

Best Time to Visit: Glacier Point is a popular spot for sunrise and sunset, as the changing light bathes the valley in golden hues. If you're up for a nighttime adventure, stargazing from Glacier Point is also a magical experience, thanks to Yosemite's clear skies and low light pollution.

Tioga Pass: Gateway to the High Sierra

Tioga Pass is the highest highway pass in California, sitting at an elevation of 9,945 feet (3,031 meters). It serves as the gateway to Yosemite's high country, offering access to stunning alpine meadows, crystal-clear lakes, and the breathtaking *Tuolumne Meadows* area. The pass connects Yosemite with the eastern Sierra and is a must-drive for those looking to explore the park's less-traveled, serene landscapes.

Scenic Highlights:

- **Olmsted Point**: A scenic viewpoint along Tioga Road where you can see sweeping views of Half Dome from a different angle and the surrounding granite domes.
- **Tenaya Lake**: A pristine alpine lake perfect for a picnic or a relaxing swim in the summer.
- **Tuolumne Meadows**: A vast, peaceful meadow surrounded by granite peaks and domes, offering plenty of hiking trails and opportunities for wildlife watching.

Seasonal Access: Tioga Pass is usually open from late May to October, depending on snowfall. During winter, the road is closed, but in the summer months, it offers a tranquil escape from the busier areas of Yosemite.

Tunnel View, Yosemite

Tunnel View: Your First Glimpse of Yosemite Valley

Tunnel View is one of the most famous and photographed viewpoints in Yosemite, offering a classic postcard-perfect view of the valley. As you emerge from the Wawona Tunnel, you're greeted with a sweeping panorama of El Capitan, Half Dome, Bridalveil Fall, and the lush Yosemite Valley below. This viewpoint provides the quintessential "welcome to Yosemite" moment for visitors arriving from the south entrance.

Best Time to Visit: Tunnel View is stunning at any time of day, but it's particularly magical at sunrise and sunset when the soft light illuminates the valley and cliffs in warm hues. Early morning offers a quieter experience with fewer crowds.

Access: Tunnel View is easily accessible by car and is located along Highway 41 (Wawona Road). There's a parking lot where you can stop, take photos, and enjoy the view.

Chapter 4

HIKING AND OUTDOOR ADVENTURES

Yosemite National Park is a hiker's paradise, offering trails that cater to all levels of fitness and experience. Whether you're looking for a gentle walk through the valley or an adrenaline-pumping adventure to the top of Half Dome, Yosemite has it all.

Day Hikes for All Levels

Easy Trails: Lower Yosemite Fall, Mirror Lake Loop

For those looking for a relaxed and scenic walk, Yosemite offers several easy trails that provide stunning views without the need for strenuous effort. These hikes are perfect for families, casual hikers, or anyone who wants to enjoy the beauty of the park at a leisurely pace.

Lower Yosemite Fall Trail

- **Distance**: 1 mile (1.6 km) round trip
- **Difficulty**: Easy
- **Elevation Gain**: Minimal

The Lower Yosemite Fall Trail is a short, easy walk that leads to the base of Yosemite Falls, one of the park's most iconic landmarks.

The paved path is accessible to all, including strollers and wheelchairs, making it a great option for families and those looking for a quick and rewarding hike. Along the way, you'll get up-close views of Lower Yosemite Fall, the final section of the tallest waterfall in North America. In the spring and early summer, the thundering water creates a cool mist that refreshes hikers as they approach the base.

Mirror Lake Loop

- **Distance**: 2 miles (3.2 km) round trip to the lake, 5 miles (8 km) for the full loop
- **Difficulty**: Easy to moderate
- **Elevation Gain**: Minimal

Mirror Lake is a peaceful spot located at the base of Half Dome, offering beautiful reflections of the surrounding cliffs. The hike to the lake is relatively easy, with a mostly flat, paved path that is great for families or those wanting a leisurely walk. For those looking for a longer hike, you can continue around the full Mirror Lake Loop, which circles the lake and provides more views of Yosemite's granite cliffs and forested areas. This trail is best in the spring and early summer when the lake is full and provides the mirror-like reflection that gives it its name.

Moderate Hikes: Mist Trail to Vernal and Nevada Falls

For hikers looking for something a bit more challenging, Yosemite's moderate trails offer a mix of stunning scenery and manageable difficulty. These hikes are perfect for those who want to experience Yosemite's waterfalls and vistas without embarking on a full-day adventure.

Mist Trail to Vernal Fall

- **Distance**: 3 miles (4.8 km) round trip to Vernal Fall
- **Difficulty**: Moderate
- **Elevation Gain**: 1,000 feet (305 meters)

The Mist Trail is one of Yosemite's most popular hikes, and for good reason. The trail takes you up close to two of the park's most beautiful waterfalls: Vernal Fall and Nevada Fall. The hike to Vernal Fall is a moderately challenging 3-mile round trip that rewards you with spectacular views of the waterfall and the surrounding granite cliffs. As you climb the stone steps alongside the waterfall, you'll be greeted with the cool mist from the falls, which can be especially refreshing on a warm day. The trail is steep in sections, but the payoff is worth it as you reach the top of Vernal Fall, where you can rest and take in the view of the rushing Merced River.

Mist Trail to Nevada Fall

- **Distance**: 7 miles (11.3 km) round trip to Nevada Fall
- **Difficulty**: Moderate to strenuous

- **Elevation Gain**: 1,900 feet (579 meters)

For those seeking more of a challenge, continue past Vernal Fall to reach **Nevada Fall**, a towering 594-foot (181-meter) waterfall that cascades into the Merced River below. The hike to Nevada Fall adds another 4 miles round trip and increases the elevation gain, making it a more strenuous adventure. However, the views from the top of Nevada Fall are truly breathtaking, offering sweeping vistas of the surrounding high country. Many hikers choose to take the **John Muir Trail** on the way back for a more gradual descent and to enjoy different views of the canyon and river.

Challenging Adventures: Hiking Half Dome, Clouds Rest

For experienced hikers and thrill-seekers, Yosemite offers some of the most challenging and rewarding day hikes in the country. These hikes require physical fitness, proper preparation, and sometimes permits, but they offer the chance to conquer some of the park's most iconic peaks.

Half Dome

- **Distance**: 14-16 miles (22-26 km) round trip
- **Difficulty**: Strenuous

- **Elevation Gain**: 4,800 feet (1,463 meters)
- **Permit Required**: Yes, for the final ascent via the cables

Hiking to the summit of **Half Dome** is a bucket-list adventure for many visitors to Yosemite. The trail is long, steep, and physically demanding, but the reward is an unforgettable view from the top of one of the park's most recognizable landmarks. The final section of the hike involves climbing the famous **Half Dome cables**, which are installed each summer to assist hikers as they ascend the sheer granite face.

The hike starts along the **Mist Trail**, passing Vernal and Nevada Falls, before continuing up through the high country toward the base of Half Dome. The final ascent up the cables is both thrilling and challenging, requiring strength, endurance, and a head for heights. Once at the summit, you'll be treated to panoramic views of Yosemite Valley, the Sierra Nevada, and beyond.

Clouds Rest

- **Distance**: 14.5 miles (23.3 km) round trip
- **Difficulty**: Strenuous
- **Elevation Gain**: 1,775 feet (541 meters)

For those looking for a less crowded alternative to Half Dome, **Clouds Rest** offers equally stunning views with fewer hikers on the trail. This challenging hike takes you to the top of one of Yosemite's highest peaks, offering a 360-degree view of the park, including a breathtaking view of Half Dome from above.

The hike to Clouds Rest starts near **Tenaya Lake** and climbs steadily through forests and meadows before reaching the narrow ridgeline that leads to the summit. The final approach involves traversing a narrow, rocky ridge with steep drop-offs on either side, so this hike is not for the faint of heart. However, the views from the top are unparalleled, with Half Dome, Yosemite Valley, and the Sierra Nevada stretching out in all directions.

Overnight and Multi-Day Treks

Yosemite National Park is home to some of the most rewarding multi-day treks in the world. For those looking to fully immerse themselves in the park's wilderness, overnight backpacking trips offer an unparalleled experience. From the famed **John Muir Trail** to the remote **High Sierra**, multi-day hikes take you deep into the park's pristine backcountry, where you can explore alpine meadows, high mountain lakes, and rugged granite peaks.

The John Muir Trail: From Yosemite to the High Sierra

The **John Muir Trail (JMT)** is one of the most famous long-distance hiking trails in the United States, stretching for 211 miles (340 km) from Yosemite Valley to **Mount Whitney**, the highest peak in the contiguous U.S. Named after the famed naturalist John Muir, the trail travels through some of the most beautiful and rugged landscapes in the Sierra Nevada, offering breathtaking views of Yosemite's granite domes, alpine lakes, and towering peaks.

While the entire trail takes about 3 weeks to complete, many hikers choose to experience shorter sections of the trail, starting in Yosemite and heading south into the High Sierra.

Key Highlights:

- Distance: 211 miles (340 km) (shorter sections can be done as multi-day trips)

- Difficulty: Strenuous (high elevation and rugged terrain)

- Elevation Gain: Total gain of over 46,000 feet (14,000 meters) for the full trail

- Permits Required: Yes, wilderness permits are required for overnight stays

Popular Sections in Yosemite:

- Yosemite Valley to Tuolumne Meadows: This is a popular 3- to 4-day section of the JMT that takes hikers from the valley floor through stunning high-country scenery. Starting at

Happy Isles in Yosemite Valley, the trail ascends past Nevada Fall, continues through Little Yosemite Valley, and eventually reaches Tuolumne Meadows, offering gorgeous views along the way.

- Tuolumne Meadows to Donohue Pass: Another popular multi-day trek, this section takes hikers deeper into the wilderness as they traverse the stunning high-altitude meadows and lakes. After passing through Lyell Canyon, hikers reach Donohue Pass, one of the highest points on the trail, where the views of the Sierra Nevada are nothing short of spectacular.

What to Expect on the JMT:

High Elevation: Much of the JMT travels through high-elevation areas, with several passes over 10,000 feet (3,000 meters). Be prepared for altitude sickness and make sure you acclimatize if you're not used to hiking at these elevations.

Remote Wilderness: The JMT is remote, so you'll need to be self-sufficient. Carry a bear canister for food storage, and be prepared to purify water from streams and lakes along the way.

Backcountry Camping: Campsites along the JMT are primitive, offering only basic amenities like flat spots for tents. You'll need to practice Leave No Trace principles, pack out all trash, and use backcountry toilets or follow wilderness waste disposal guidelines.

For those planning to hike the entire John Muir Trail, it's essential to obtain the proper permits, which are highly competitive, especially for the Yosemite section. Apply as early as possible and be flexible with your start date to increase your chances of securing a permit.

Yosemite for Families

Yosemite National Park is not only a haven for adventurers and nature lovers but also a fantastic destination for families. The park offers a range of activities and hikes that are perfectly suited for children, making it an ideal place for family trips. Whether you're introducing your kids to hiking or looking for fun and educational activities, Yosemite provides countless opportunities to create lasting memories together.

Kid-Friendly Hikes and Activities

Yosemite is full of easy and accessible trails that allow children to enjoy the park's natural beauty without the challenge of steep terrain or long distances. Here are some of the best kid-friendly hikes and activities:

Lower Yosemite Fall Trail

- **Distance**: 1 mile (1.6 km) round trip

- **Difficulty**: Easy

- **Elevation Gain**: Minimal

This short and easy trail is perfect for families with young children. The paved path leads to the base of **Lower Yosemite Fall**, one of the most impressive waterfalls in the park. Kids will love the roar of the falls and the cool mist that fills the air. Along the way, there are educational signs about the park's geology and ecosystems, making it a great learning experience. The trail is stroller-friendly and accessible, making it suitable for all ages.

Mirror Lake Loop

- **Distance**: 2 miles (3.2 km) round trip to the lake, 5 miles (8 km) for the full loop

- **Difficulty**: Easy

- **Elevation Gain**: Minimal

Mirror Lake offers a peaceful and relatively flat walk that's perfect for families. The short 2-mile hike to the lake provides beautiful views of the surrounding granite cliffs, including **Half Dome**. Kids will enjoy the opportunity to splash around in the water (seasonally) or explore the sandy shores. The trail is mostly paved, making it accessible for strollers. In the spring and early summer, the lake is full and reflects the towering cliffs, creating stunning photo opportunities.

Bridalveil Fall Trail

- **Distance**: 0.5 miles (0.8 km) round trip

- **Difficulty**: Easy

- **Elevation Gain**: Minimal

The Bridalveil Fall Trail is one of the shortest and easiest walks in Yosemite, making it perfect for young children. The trail leads to the base of **Bridalveil Fall**, where the mist from the waterfall often creates rainbows on sunny days. The short walk is shaded, and the sound of the rushing water makes the trail feel magical for little ones. It's a great spot for a quick family adventure.

Happy Isles Nature Center

If you're looking for a fun and educational stop, head to the **Happy Isles Nature Center** in Yosemite Valley. This center offers interactive exhibits about the park's ecosystems, animals, and geology, making it a great place for kids to learn about nature. The surrounding area features short trails and outdoor play spaces where children can explore the natural environment. Rangers often hold kid-friendly programs, including storytelling, nature walks, and hands-on activities.

Junior Ranger Program

Yosemite's **Junior Ranger Program** is an excellent way for kids to engage with the park in a fun and meaningful way. The program is designed for children ages 7 to 13 but can be enjoyed by younger kids with parental assistance. To participate, children's complete activities in a special workbook that teaches them about the park's wildlife, history, and conservation efforts. Once they complete the workbook, they take an oath to protect the park and receive an official Junior Ranger badge.

Yosemite Valley Stables

For a unique experience, families can take part in guided horseback rides at the **Yosemite Valley Stables**. Children over 7 years old can join these trail rides, which offer a different way to explore the park's meadows and forests. For younger kids or those not comfortable riding, there are shorter pony rides available.

Tips for Exploring with Children

Exploring Yosemite with children can be a rewarding experience, but it requires some extra planning and preparation to ensure the whole family has a safe and enjoyable time. Here are some tips to make the most of your Yosemite adventure with kids:

Choose Age-Appropriate Hikes

When hiking with children, it's important to choose trails that match their abilities and energy levels. Stick to shorter, easier trails like the ones mentioned above, and avoid hikes with steep inclines or long distances unless your kids are experienced hikers. Be mindful of elevation changes, as younger children may tire more quickly at higher altitudes.

Take Frequent Breaks

Kids may need more frequent breaks than adults, especially on longer hikes. Allow time for rest stops where children can snack, drink water, or explore the environment around them. Bring plenty of water and snacks to keep everyone energized.

Pack Light but Smart

When hiking with children, it's important to pack essentials without overloading your backpack. Bring sun protection (hats, sunscreen, sunglasses), plenty of water, snacks, and an extra layer of clothing, as temperatures can fluctuate throughout the day. For younger children, do not forget diapers, wipes, and a small first-aid kit for minor scrapes or injuries.

Encourage Nature Exploration

Yosemite is the perfect place for kids to explore and discover nature. Bring binoculars for birdwatching, a magnifying glass for examining plants and insects, or a small notebook where kids can draw or write about what they see. Encourage them to observe the surroundings, listen to the sounds of the forest, and ask questions about the animals, plants, and rocks they encounter.

Plan Around Nap Times

If you are visiting with younger children who still need naps, plan your day around their schedule. Early mornings or late afternoons can be great times to explore when the park is quieter and cooler. You can also bring a stroller or child carrier for longer walks, allowing little ones to rest while you continue to explore.

Keep Safety in Mind

Yosemite is home to wildlife, including black bears, deer, and squirrels. Teach your children the importance of respecting wildlife by observing animals from a distance and never feeding them.

Additionally, remind kids to stay on marked trails and be cautious near water, as rivers and waterfalls can have strong currents. Always supervise children closely, especially in areas with steep drop-offs or slippery surfaces.

Be Available for Play

Children need time to play and burn off energy. Yosemite has plenty of open spaces, meadows, and picnic areas where kids can run around, explore, and simply enjoy being in nature. Take advantage of these spots to let your kids play freely, whether it's skipping stones in a stream, playing in the sand at Mirror Lake, or having a family picnic.

Capture the Memories

Bring a camera or let older kids take photos of their favorite moments in Yosemite. Capturing family memories can be a fun way to engage children in the experience and gives them a chance to reflect on their adventure. You can also encourage them to keep a travel journal or scrapbook to document the animals, plants, and landscapes they encounter.

Chapter 5

OUTDOOR ACTIVITIES BEYOND HIKING

While hiking is one of the most popular ways to explore Yosemite, the park offers a wide variety of other outdoor activities that let you experience its natural wonders from different perspectives. From rock climbing and water sports to wildlife watching and photography, Yosemite is a haven for adventurers and nature enthusiasts alike.

Rock Climbing and Bouldering

Yosemite National Park is one of the world's most famous destinations for rock climbing, drawing climbers from all over the globe to test their skills on its legendary granite walls. Whether you're an experienced climber looking to tackle a world-class route or a beginner wanting to learn the ropes, Yosemite has something to offer.

Where Beginners Can Learn to Climb

If you are new to rock climbing but want to experience Yosemite's climbing culture, there are several opportunities to get started. Yosemite offers climbing schools and guides that provide instruction for beginners, teaching essential skills in a safe and supportive environment.

Yosemite Mountaineering School: Located in Yosemite Valley, the Yosemite Mountaineering School offers guided climbs and courses for all levels, from beginners to advanced climbers. You can start with an introductory half-day class to learn the basics of climbing technique, belaying, and safety. For those looking to gain more experience, full-day and multi-day classes are available.

Bouldering at Camp 4: For a more independent experience, beginners can try their hand at bouldering in Yosemite's **Camp 4** area. With a wide range of problems for different skill levels, Camp 4 offers a great introduction to climbing without the need for ropes or complex equipment. Be sure to bring climbing shoes and chalk for grip.

Rafting and Kayaking on the Merced River

During the summer, the **Merced River** becomes a hub for water sports, offering a relaxing way to see the valley from a new perspective. The gentle currents of the river make it ideal for families and visitors looking to cool off while taking in the scenery.

Rafting: One of the most popular activities on the Merced River is rafting. You can rent a raft from vendors in Yosemite Valley and float along a scenic 3-mile stretch of the river. The ride takes you past iconic landmarks like **El Capitan** and **Half Dome**, with plenty of opportunities to stop and picnic along the riverbanks.

Kayaking: If you prefer a more active adventure, you can rent a kayak and paddle down the Merced River. Kayaking gives you more control and allows you to explore quieter sections of the river, away from the busier rafting routes.

Best Time to Raft or Kayak: The Merced River is typically best for rafting and kayaking from late June through August, when water levels are high enough to support these activities. Early in the season, the river can be too fast and dangerous for recreational use, so always check with park rangers for current conditions.

Fishing in Yosemite: Top Spots and Regulations

Fishing is another peaceful way to connect with Yosemite's natural environment. The park's rivers, streams, and lakes are home to a variety of fish, including rainbow and brown trout.

Top Fishing Spots:

Merced River: The Merced River offers excellent fishing opportunities, particularly in the **Merced Lake** area and along stretches near **Yosemite Valley**. The river is stocked with trout, and fly fishing is especially popular here.

Tuolumne River: For those exploring the high country, the **Tuolumne River** in **Tuolumne Meadows** provides great fishing in a pristine alpine setting. The river's clear, cold waters are home to both rainbow and brown trout.

Tenaya Lake: This beautiful alpine lake offers peaceful fishing in the high country, with stunning views of the surrounding granite peaks.

Fishing Regulations:

A valid California fishing license is required for anyone 16 years or older.

Fishing season in Yosemite typically runs from late April to mid-November, though some areas may have restrictions or closures due to wildlife protection.

Catch-and-release fishing is encouraged to preserve fish populations, and specific limits on the number and size of fish may apply in certain areas.

Always check with park authorities for the latest regulations and guidelines.

Wildlife Watching and Photography

Yosemite is home to a diverse range of wildlife, making it a fantastic destination for wildlife watching and photography. From black bears and mule deer to a wide variety of bird species, the park offers countless opportunities to observe and capture the beauty of its natural inhabitants.

Best Times and Places to Spot Bears, Deer, and Birds

Black Bears: Yosemite is famous for its black bear population, and while sightings are more common in remote areas, bears can occasionally be seen in Yosemite Valley as well. The best times to spot bears are in the early morning or late evening when they are most active. Bears are often found in meadows or foraging near berry bushes.

Best places to see bears: Tuolumne Meadows, Mariposa Grove, and Glacier Point Road.

Mule Deer: Mule deer are a common sight in Yosemite, and you're likely to spot them grazing in meadows or wandering through the forest. They are especially visible in Yosemite Valley and the surrounding areas. Like bears, they are most active during the early morning and late afternoon.

Best places to see deer: Yosemite Valley, Wawona Meadow, and Big Trees Lodge.

Birdwatching: Yosemite is home to more than 250 species of birds, making it a birdwatcher's paradise. Some of the most sought-after species include the **peregrine falcon, great gray owl**, and **Steller's jay.** Spring and early summer are the best times for birdwatching, as migratory species return to the park.

Best places for birdwatching: Mariposa Grove, Tuolumne Meadows, and the Merced River.

Tips for Capturing Yosemite's Natural Beauty Through Your Lens

Yosemite's dramatic landscapes and abundant wildlife make it a dream destination for photographers. Whether you're shooting the iconic granite cliffs or focusing on the park's wildlife, here are some tips to help you capture the essence of Yosemite.

- **Golden Hours**: The best light for photography in Yosemite is during the "golden hours" — the period just after sunrise and before sunset. During these times, the soft light enhances the colors of the granite cliffs and meadows, creating stunning natural contrasts. **Tunnel View, Glacier Point**, and **Valley View** are especially beautiful at sunrise and sunset.

- **Use a Telephoto Lens for Wildlife**: To safely capture images of animals like black bears and deer, a telephoto lens is essential. This allows you to photograph wildlife from a distance without disturbing the animals or putting yourself at risk.

- **Focus on Reflections**: Yosemite's rivers and lakes, especially **Mirror Lake** and the **Merced River**, provide excellent opportunities for capturing reflections of the surrounding cliffs and trees. Use a tripod to stabilize your camera and try shooting in the early morning when the water is calm.

- **Plan for Weather**: Yosemite's weather can change quickly, and dramatic clouds, fog, or storms can add a unique and moody feel to your photos. Be prepared for these conditions and use them to your advantage by capturing the park's ever-changing atmosphere.

- **Night Sky Photography**: Yosemite's dark skies are perfect for night photography, especially if you want to capture the

Milky Way or do some star trails. **Glacier Point** and **Olmsted Point** offer wide-open views of the night sky, free from light pollution.

My Best Spot for Photo Location

Chapter 6

HIDDEN GEMS AND OFF-THE-BEATEN-PATH ADVENTURES

Yosemite National Park is world-renowned for its iconic landmarks, but beyond the famous sights like Yosemite Valley and Half Dome, the park is filled with hidden gems and quieter adventures. For those looking to escape the crowds and experience Yosemite's more peaceful and secluded areas, this chapter will guide you to lesser-known trails, secret waterfalls, and nearby destinations that offer a more intimate connection with nature.

Lesser-Known Trails and Secluded Spots

For those who want to explore Yosemite away from the more tourist-heavy areas, the park has plenty of quieter, lesser-known spots that offer incredible scenery and solitude. These areas allow you to enjoy Yosemite's beauty without the crowds.

Discovering Hetch Hetchy

The Quieter Yosemite Valley

Often called the "forgotten Yosemite Valley," **Hetch Hetchy** is a hidden gem located in the northwestern part of the park. This area features stunning granite cliffs, cascading waterfalls, and a large reservoir surrounded by beautiful wilderness, yet it receives far fewer visitors than the main Yosemite Valley.

Hetch Hetchy Reservoir was created by the O'Shaughnessy Dam, which provides water for the city of San Francisco. While the reservoir altered the natural landscape, Hetch Hetchy still offers some of Yosemite's most beautiful scenery, especially in spring when waterfalls like **Wapama Falls** and **Tueeulala Falls** are at their peak.

Top Trails in Hetch Hetchy:

- **Wapama Falls Trail**: A 5-mile (8 km) round trip hike along the reservoir to one of the area's most powerful waterfalls. The trail is relatively easy and offers stunning views of the surrounding granite cliffs.

- **Rancheria Falls**: For a more challenging adventure, hike the 13-mile (21 km) round trip trail to **Rancheria Falls**. This hike takes you deeper into the wilderness and rewards you with a peaceful waterfall and a sense of isolation.

Why Visit Hetch Hetchy: If you're looking for a place to escape the crowds of Yosemite Valley, Hetch Hetchy offers a quieter, more serene experience with equally stunning landscapes.

Tuolumne Meadows: High Sierra Solitude

Located in Yosemite's high country, **Tuolumne Meadows** offers a completely different experience from the bustling Yosemite Valley. At an elevation of 8,600 feet (2,621 meters), Tuolumne Meadows is a vast expanse of alpine meadows surrounded by granite domes and the winding Tuolumne River. The meadows are a perfect place for peaceful hiking, wildlife watching, and stargazing.

Top Trails in Tuolumne Meadows:

- **Glen Aulin Trail**: A 13-mile (21 km) round trip hike that takes you along the Tuolumne River to the Glen Aulin High Sierra Camp and waterfall. This trail offers incredible views of alpine scenery and is less crowded than trails in Yosemite Valley.

- **Cathedral Lakes Trail**: A 7-mile (11 km) round trip hike that leads to two stunning alpine lakes, offering crystal-clear waters and magnificent views of the surrounding peaks.

Why Visit Tuolumne Meadows: If you're looking for solitude and the beauty of Yosemite's high country, Tuolumne Meadows is the perfect escape. The area is typically less crowded, even during peak season, and offers cooler temperatures in the summer.

Wawona: History and Charm in Southern Yosemite

Located in the southern part of Yosemite, **Wawona** is a historic area known for its peaceful atmosphere, beautiful meadows, and charming 19th-century architecture. Wawona was one of the earliest tourist destinations in Yosemite, and it remains a quiet retreat for visitors today.

Things to See in Wawona:

- **Pioneer Yosemite History Center**: This open-air museum showcases historic cabins, wagons, and structures from Yosemite's early days. Kids and history buffs alike will enjoy learning about Yosemite's pioneer past and its development as a national park.

- **Chilnualna Falls Trail**: One of the hidden gems of Wawona, the **Chilnualna Falls Trail** is a 8.2-mile (13.2 km) round trip hike that leads to a series of cascading waterfalls. The trail is moderately challenging, but it offers solitude and stunning views of the falls.

- **Wawona Meadow Loop**: This 3.5-mile (5.6 km) loop is a gentle and scenic hike around Wawona Meadow, perfect for families or those looking for a peaceful walk in nature.

Why Visit Wawona: Wawona offers a slower pace and a rich sense of history. Its secluded trails, charming accommodations, and proximity to the **Mariposa Grove of Giant Sequoias** make it a great destination for those seeking a quiet retreat.

Yosemite's Secret Waterfalls

Yosemite is famous for its waterfalls, but beyond the well-known giants like Yosemite Falls and Bridalveil Fall, the park is home to many lesser-known waterfalls that are just as beautiful and far less crowded.

Chilnualna Falls: Hidden Cascade in Wawona

Located in the Wawona area, **Chilnualna Falls** is one of Yosemite's hidden gems. The waterfall is a series of cascades that drop nearly 2,200 feet (670 meters) along Chilnualna Creek. The hike to the falls is moderately challenging but offers beautiful views of the surrounding wilderness.

Trail Information:

- **Distance**: 8.2 miles (13.2 km) round trip

- **Difficulty**: Moderate to strenuous

- **Elevation Gain**: 2,400 feet (731 meters)

Unlike the more famous Yosemite Valley waterfalls, Chilnualna Falls sees far fewer visitors, making it a great choice for hikers seeking solitude. The falls are particularly beautiful in the spring when the water flow is at its peak.

Ribbon Fall: Yosemite's Tallest Secret

Ribbon Fall is one of the tallest waterfalls in Yosemite, plunging 1,612 feet (491 meters) off the western side of El Capitan. Despite its impressive height, Ribbon Fall is one of the park's lesser-known waterfalls because it is only visible from certain vantage points, and its flow is highly seasonal, typically drying up by summer.

Best Viewing Spot: The best place to view Ribbon Fall is from **Southside Drive** in Yosemite Valley, near Bridalveil Fall. The fall is most active in early spring, fed by snowmelt.

Chapter 7

PRACTICAL TIPS FOR YOUR VISIT

A trip to Yosemite National Park is an adventure filled with stunning landscapes, exciting activities, and opportunities to explore the beauty of nature. However, to make sure your visit is both enjoyable and safe, it's important to be aware of potential hazards and prepare accordingly. This chapter covers essential tips to ensure you stay safe while exploring Yosemite's diverse environments, from wildlife encounters to the challenges of high-altitude hiking.

Staying Safe in Yosemite

Yosemite is a natural wonder, but with its vast wilderness and variety of wildlife, it's essential to be prepared. Here are some tips to help you stay safe during your visit.

Wildlife Safety: Bears, Snakes, and Other Critters

Yosemite is home to a wide variety of wildlife, including black bears, mule deer, coyotes, and several species of snakes. While it's exciting to see animals in their natural habitat, it's crucial to understand how to safely interact (or not interact) with wildlife to protect both yourself and the animals.

Black Bears

Black bears are one of the most famous animals in Yosemite, and while they are generally not aggressive toward humans, improper food storage and close encounters can lead to dangerous situations. Here's how to stay safe around bears:

Store Food Properly: Bears have an excellent sense of smell and are drawn to food and scented items. All food, toiletries, and trash must be stored in bear-proof lockers (available at campsites) or bear canisters if you're backpacking. Never leave food unattended in your car or tent.

Do Not Approach: If you see a bear in the wild, observe it from a distance. Stay at least 100 yards away. If a bear approaches, make noise to scare it away—clap your hands, yell, or bang on pots and pans. Never run from a bear, as this may trigger a chase response.

Encountering a Bear: If you encounter a bear while hiking, make yourself look larger by raising your arms and speaking loudly. Slowly back away and give the bear plenty of space to retreat.

Snakes

Yosemite is home to several species of snakes, including the northern Pacific rattlesnake, the park's only venomous snake. Most snakes are shy and will avoid human contact, but it's important to know what to do if you encounter one.

Watch Your Step: Snakes are often found sunning themselves on rocks or hiding in tall grass. Stay on marked trails, and avoid reaching into brush or crevices where snakes may be hiding.

Rattlesnake Safety: If you hear a rattlesnake's warning rattle, stop immediately and slowly move away. Rattlesnakes only bite in self-defense, so giving them space is the best way to avoid an incident.

First Aid for Snakebites: In the rare event of a rattlesnake bite, remain calm and call for help. Do not try to suck out the venom or apply a tourniquet. Keep the bitten limb immobilized and lower than the heart while waiting for medical assistance.

Other Critters

Smaller animals like squirrels, raccoons, and coyotes are common in Yosemite. While they may seem harmless, it's essential not to feed or approach these animals.

Do Not Feed Wildlife: Feeding animals disrupts their natural behaviors and can make them dependent on humans for food. It can also lead to aggressive behavior toward visitors. Keep all food securely stored, and never offer food to wild animals.

Tick and Insect Awareness: Ticks are common in grassy and wooded areas and can transmit diseases like Lyme disease. Use insect repellent, wear long sleeves and pants, and check yourself for ticks after hiking. If you find a tick attached to your skin, remove it with tweezers and clean the area thoroughly.

Staying Hydrated and Avoiding Altitude Sickness

Yosemite's beautiful landscapes are accompanied by diverse elevations, ranging from the valley floor at around 4,000 feet to high-country peaks over 10,000 feet. Staying hydrated and managing altitude changes are key to a safe and enjoyable visit.

Staying Hydrated

Dehydration is a common risk when hiking or spending extended periods outdoors, especially during the summer months when temperatures can rise, and the sun is strong.

Carry Plenty of Water: Always bring enough water with you when hiking, and remember that higher elevations can increase your body's need for hydration. For day hikes, aim to carry at least 2 liters (half a gallon) of water per person. For longer hikes or multi-day treks, bring extra water or a water purification method (such as a filter or purification tablets) to treat water from streams or rivers.

Start Early: Hiking in the early morning or late afternoon when the temperatures are cooler can help you avoid dehydration during the hottest part of the day. Take regular breaks and find shade to rest when necessary.

Recognize Signs of Dehydration: Symptoms of dehydration include dry mouth, dizziness, fatigue, and headache. If you notice any of these signs, stop and drink water immediately.

Avoiding Altitude Sickness

For visitors exploring Yosemite's high country—such as **Tuolumne Meadows**, **Glacier Point**, or trails like **Half Dome**—altitude sickness can be a concern. Altitude sickness occurs when your body struggles to adjust to lower oxygen levels at higher elevations.

Acclimatize Slowly: If you're coming from sea level or lower elevations, give your body time to adjust to the altitude. Start with shorter hikes and gradually work your way up to higher elevations.

Stay Hydrated: Drinking plenty of water can help your body adjust to the altitude. Avoid alcohol and caffeine, which can contribute to dehydration.

Know the Symptoms: Common symptoms of altitude sickness include headache, nausea, dizziness, and shortness of breath. If you experience these symptoms, descend to a lower elevation and rest. In severe cases, seek medical attention.

Take Breaks: Hiking at high altitudes can be more physically demanding, so take breaks often and listen to your body. Don't push yourself too hard, especially if you're feeling fatigued.

First Aid Kits and Emergency Preparedness

It's always a good idea to carry a small first aid kit when exploring Yosemite. Include band-aids, antiseptic wipes, pain relievers, blister treatment, and any personal medications. Make sure someone in your group knows basic first aid and be familiar with Yosemite's emergency contact procedures.

Chapter 8

FOOD AND DINING IN YOSEMITE

After a long day of hiking, sightseeing, or exploring Yosemite's stunning landscapes, you'll likely be ready for a good meal. Whether you're looking for a quick bite, a sit-down restaurant, or a place to stock up on groceries for a picnic or campfire meal, Yosemite offers a variety of dining options to suit all tastes and budgets. In this chapter, we'll explore the best places to eat and where to find supplies during your visit to the park.

Where to Eat: Cafes, Restaurants, and Grocery Stores

Yosemite has several dining options, ranging from casual cafes and fast food to more upscale dining experiences. Most of these can be found in Yosemite Valley, but there are also a few options in other areas of the park, including Wawona, Tuolumne Meadows, and nearby towns.

Restaurants and Cafes

The Ahwahnee Dining Room

- **Location**: The Ahwahnee Hotel, Yosemite Valley
- **Type**: Fine dining

- **Cuisine:** American and international cuisine

- **Hours:** Breakfast, lunch, dinner, and Sunday brunch

For an upscale dining experience in Yosemite, **The Ahwahnee Dining Room** offers a majestic setting with high ceilings, large windows, and views of the surrounding cliffs. The menu features American classics with a touch of sophistication, including dishes like seared salmon, roast duck, and prime rib. There are also vegetarian and gluten-free options available. Reservations are recommended, especially for dinner and Sunday brunch.

Yosemite Valley Lodge – Base Camp Eatery

- **Location:** Yosemite Valley Lodge, Yosemite Valley

- **Type:** Casual dining

- **Cuisine:** American, fast food

- **Hours:** Breakfast, lunch, and dinner

If you're looking for a quick and casual meal, the **Base Camp Eatery** at Yosemite Valley Lodge is a convenient option. The menu includes classic American fare like burgers, pizza, salads, and sandwiches, as well as some vegetarian and gluten-free options. It's a great place to grab a meal before or after exploring the valley.

- **Location**: Curry Village, Yosemite Valley
- **Type**: Casual dining
- **Cuisine**: Pizza and bar food
- **Hours**: Lunch and dinner

For a family-friendly and budget-friendly dining option, head to the **Pizza Deck** in Curry Village. The outdoor seating area offers a relaxed atmosphere with views of the valley, and the menu features a variety of pizzas, salads, and cold beverages. There's also a small bar nearby where you can grab a drink and unwind after a day of adventure.

Degnan's Kitchen

- **Location**: Yosemite Village, Yosemite Valley
- **Type**: Café
- **Cuisine**: Coffee, sandwiches, bakery items
- **Hours**: Breakfast and lunch

Degnan's Kitchen is a popular spot in Yosemite Village for a quick breakfast, lunch, or snack. The café serves coffee, pastries, sandwiches, salads, and grab-and-go items, making it a great choice if you're looking for something light before hitting the trails. There's also outdoor seating where you can enjoy your meal with a view of Yosemite's iconic scenery.

Grocery Stores and General Stores

Yosemite Village Store

- **Location**: Yosemite Village, Yosemite Valley
- **Type**: Grocery and general store

If you're planning to cook your own meals or need to stock up on snacks, the **Yosemite Village Store** is the best place to find groceries in the valley. The store carries a wide range of items, including fresh produce, packaged snacks, canned goods, beverages, and camping essentials. There's also a small selection of souvenirs and outdoor gear if you need any last-minute items for your trip.

Curry Village Gift & Grocery

- **Location**: Curry Village, Yosemite Valley
- **Type**: Grocery and general store

The **Curry Village Gift & Grocery** store offers a smaller selection of groceries, but it's a convenient option for those staying in or near Curry Village. You'll find basic food supplies, snacks, and drinks, as well as some camping gear and souvenirs. It's a good spot to grab a quick snack or replenish supplies before heading out on a hike.

Wawona Store & Pioneer Gift Shop

- **Location**: Wawona, Southern Yosemite
- **Type**: Grocery and general store

If you're staying in the southern part of the park, the **Wawona Store** offers a variety of grocery items, snacks, and camping supplies. The store also has a selection of local gifts and souvenirs. It's a great stop if you're visiting the **Mariposa Grove** or spending time in the quieter Wawona area.

Dining Options Outside Yosemite

For those staying outside the park or looking for more dining options, the nearby towns of **Mariposa**, **El Portal**, and **Groveland** offer a range of restaurants and grocery stores. These locations can be especially useful if you're entering or leaving the park through one of the main entrances.

El Portal Market

- **Location**: El Portal, just outside Yosemite's Arch Rock Entrance
- **Type**: Grocery and general store

Located just outside the Arch Rock Entrance, the **El Portal Market** is a convenient place to stock up on groceries and supplies before entering the park. The store offers fresh produce, snacks, drinks, and basic camping gear. It's a great stop if you need to pick up food for a picnic or prepare for a multi-day stay in the park.

The River Restaurant & Lounge

- **Location**: El Portal

- **Type**: Casual dining

- **Cuisine**: American and international cuisine

Located just outside Yosemite in El Portal, **The River Restaurant & Lounge** offers a relaxing dining experience with views of the Merced River. The menu includes a mix of American and international dishes, such as steaks, burgers, pasta, and seafood. It's a great place to unwind after a day of exploring the park, and the outdoor patio provides a scenic backdrop for your meal.

Picnic Spots and Outdoor Dining Options

One of the best ways to enjoy Yosemite National Park's stunning landscapes is by having a picnic surrounded by nature. With countless scenic spots offering breathtaking views, picnic areas in Yosemite provide a peaceful and relaxing way to enjoy a meal outdoors. Whether you're taking a break during a hike or simply soaking in the natural beauty, Yosemite's picnic spots are perfect for a leisurely outdoor meal. This section highlights some of the best places for picnicking and outdoor dining in Yosemite.

Top Picnic Spots in Yosemite

Cathedral Beach Picnic Area

- **Location**: Yosemite Valley
- **Facilities**: Picnic tables, grills, restrooms, river access

The **Cathedral Beach Picnic Area** is one of the most picturesque picnic spots in Yosemite Valley. Located along the banks of the **Merced River**, this area offers stunning views of **El Capitan** and a peaceful setting for a picnic. There are picnic tables and grills available, making it a great spot to enjoy a meal while surrounded by towering granite cliffs and serene river views. Cathedral Beach also provides access to the river, so you can relax by the water or take a dip on warm days.

Sentinel Beach Picnic Area

- **Location**: Yosemite Valley
- **Facilities**: Picnic tables, grills, restrooms, river access

Another fantastic spot along the Merced River is the **Sentinel Beach Picnic Area**. This location offers a peaceful setting with views of **Sentinel Rock** and **Half Dome** in the distance. The picnic area is equipped with tables, grills, and restrooms, making it a convenient place for families and groups to gather. You can also enjoy easy access to the river for wading or simply relaxing by the water. Sentinel Beach is less crowded than some of the other picnic spots, making it a good choice if you're seeking a quieter experience.

Bridalveil Fall Picnic Area

- **Location**: Near Bridalveil Fall
- **Facilities**: Picnic tables, restrooms

If you're visiting **Bridalveil Fall**, the nearby picnic area offers a convenient place to enjoy a meal. Located just a short walk from the trailhead, this picnic area features tables and restrooms, making it an easy stop for lunch before or after viewing the falls. Although the picnic area itself doesn't offer direct views of the waterfall, the sounds of Bridalveil Fall can still be heard in the distance, adding to the peaceful ambiance.

Tenaya Lake Picnic Area

- **Location**: Tioga Road, Tuolumne Meadows
- **Facilities**: Picnic tables, restrooms, lake access

If you're exploring Yosemite's high country along Tioga Road, the Tenaya Lake Picnic Area is a must-visit spot. Located on the shores of Tenaya Lake, this picnic area offers breathtaking views of the clear, alpine lake and the surrounding granite domes. There are picnic tables and restrooms available, and the lake provides a perfect setting for swimming, kayaking, or simply relaxing by the water. It's an ideal stop for those traveling through Tuolumne Meadows and seeking a peaceful, scenic picnic spot.

Wawona Meadow Loop Picnic Area

- **Location**: Wawona, Southern Yosemite
- **Facilities**: Picnic tables, restrooms

For visitors staying in or near Wawona, the Wawona Meadow Loop offers a beautiful and less-crowded spot for a picnic. The picnic area is located along the peaceful Wawona Meadow, where you can enjoy views of the surrounding forest and mountains. Picnic tables and restrooms are available, and the nearby Wawona Hotel offers a historic backdrop for your outdoor meal. After your picnic, you can take a leisurely walk along the Wawona Meadow Loop Trail, a 3.5-mile (5.6 km) trail that circles the meadow.

Outdoor Dining Options

If you prefer outdoor dining without packing a picnic, several dining establishments in Yosemite offer beautiful outdoor seating areas where you can enjoy your meal with a view.

Curry Village Pavilion

- **Location**: Curry Village, Yosemite Valley
- **Facilities**: Outdoor seating, food court

The Curry Village Pavilion offers a food court with a variety of quick-service options, including pizza, burgers, and salads. There's a large outdoor seating area where you can enjoy your meal while taking in the views of the surrounding cliffs and trees. This is a great option for those staying in Curry Village or looking for a casual meal with outdoor seating in Yosemite Valley.

The Ahwahnee Bar and Outdoor Patio

- **Location**: The Ahwahnee Hotel, Yosemite Valley
- **Facilities**: Outdoor patio seating, full-service bar

For a more upscale outdoor dining experience, head to the Ahwahnee Bar at The Ahwahnee Hotel. The bar offers light bites, sandwiches, and drinks, and you can enjoy your meal on the outdoor patio, which features stunning views of the hotel's gardens and the granite cliffs beyond. It's a relaxing and elegant spot to unwind after a day of exploring the park.

Degnan's Kitchen

- **Location**: Yosemite Village, Yosemite Valley
- **Facilities**: Outdoor seating, café

Degnan's Kitchen offers a variety of grab-and-go items like sandwiches, salads, and pastries, perfect for a quick meal. The outdoor seating area provides a relaxed environment where you can enjoy your food while soaking in the sights and sounds of Yosemite Village. It's an ideal stop for a casual breakfast or lunch before setting off on a hike or exploring nearby attractions.

Chapter 9

SUSTAINABILITY AND RESPONSIBLE TRAVEL

Yosemite National Park is one of the most pristine natural environments in the world, but with millions of visitors each year, it's essential to protect the park's delicate ecosystems. Being a responsible traveler helps ensure that future generations can enjoy Yosemite's breathtaking beauty. In this chapter, we'll discuss how you can minimize your impact on the environment, respect wildlife, and contribute to the park's sustainability efforts.

How to Be a Responsible Traveler

Visiting Yosemite comes with a responsibility to care for the park and its fragile ecosystems. By practicing sustainability and being mindful of your actions, you can help preserve Yosemite for future visitors.

Leave No Trace: Minimizing Your Impact on the Environment

One of the most important principles for any visitor to Yosemite is to follow the **Leave No Trace** principles. These guidelines are designed to help people minimize their impact on the environment while enjoying the park's beauty.

The Seven Leave No Trace Principles:

1. **Plan Ahead and Prepare**: Research your trip in advance to ensure you're prepared for the terrain, weather, and regulations in Yosemite. Having the right gear and knowledge will help reduce your impact on the environment.

2. **Travel and Camp on Durable Surfaces**: Stick to designated trails and campsites to prevent damaging fragile vegetation and disturbing wildlife habitats. Avoid creating new trails or campsites, as this can lead to erosion and habitat destruction.

3. **Dispose of Waste Properly**: Pack out all of your trash, including food scraps and biodegradable items. Never leave litter behind, even in remote areas. Use designated trash and recycling bins when available, and if you're in the backcountry, carry a small trash bag with you to collect any waste.

4. **Leave What You Find**: Avoid picking plants, collecting rocks, or disturbing natural or cultural features. Yosemite is home to unique ecosystems, and leaving things as you found them helps preserve the park's natural and cultural heritage.

5. **Minimize Campfire Impact**: In Yosemite, campfires are only allowed in designated areas, and even then, they should be kept small. Use established fire rings and avoid collecting wood from the environment. Always fully extinguish your fire before leaving.

6. **Respect Wildlife**: Observe animals from a distance and never feed them. Feeding wildlife can disrupt their natural behavior and diet, leading to dependency on human food, which can harm their health and safety.

7. **Be Considerate of Other Visitors**: Yosemite is a shared space, so be mindful of other visitors by keeping noise levels low, respecting others' space, and being courteous on trails.

By adhering to these principles, you can help ensure that Yosemite remains a place of beauty and wonder for generations to come.

Respect Wildlife and Natural Habitats

Yosemite is home to a diverse range of wildlife, from black bears and mule deer to birds, reptiles, and smaller creatures. Respecting these animals and their habitats is crucial for their well-being and for maintaining the park's ecological balance.

How to Respect Wildlife:

- **Keep a Safe Distance**: Always observe wildlife from a distance. Yosemite recommends staying at least 100 yards away from bears and 25 yards away from all other wildlife. Getting too close can stress animals and cause them to behave unpredictably.

- **Do Not Feed Wildlife**: Feeding wildlife is harmful to their health and can make them dependent on human food.

Once animals associate humans with food, they may become aggressive or habituated, which often leads to dangerous situations and can result in animals being relocated or euthanized.

- **Keep the Environment Clean**: Animals can be drawn to food scraps and trash left behind by visitors. Always clean up after yourself and use bear-proof containers to store food in camping areas.

- **Stay on Trails**: Venturing off-trail can disturb sensitive habitats and wildlife, especially during breeding or nesting seasons. Stick to established paths to protect the environment and avoid trampling on plants or disturbing animals.

Yosemite's Conservation Efforts

Yosemite National Park is actively involved in numerous conservation and sustainability initiatives to preserve its unique landscapes, ecosystems, and wildlife. These efforts help protect the park's natural beauty while ensuring it remains resilient in the face of challenges such as climate change, increasing visitor numbers, and environmental degradation.

How the Park is Managed to Preserve Its Beauty

Yosemite's management focuses on maintaining a balance between providing access to visitors and protecting the park's ecosystems. The **National Park Service (NPS)**, which oversees

Yosemite, implements a variety of strategies to minimize human impact while maintaining the park's natural beauty.

Key Conservation Initiatives:

Wildlife Management: Yosemite's wildlife management programs aim to protect species from harm, maintain natural habitats, and ensure healthy populations. This includes efforts to monitor and protect black bears, restore habitats for endangered species, and manage human-wildlife interactions.

Restoration Projects: Several areas of Yosemite have undergone habitat restoration to repair damage caused by human activity, invasive species, and erosion. Projects like the **Merced River Restoration** work to restore the river's natural flow and improve riparian habitats, while efforts in **Tuolumne Meadows** aim to protect its delicate alpine ecosystems.

Fire Management: Yosemite uses controlled burns and other fire management practices to reduce the risk of large, destructive wildfires. Fire plays a natural role in many of the park's ecosystems, promoting new growth and maintaining the health of forests. Controlled burns help replicate this natural process while protecting the park's infrastructure and visitors.

Visitor Management: Yosemite has implemented several measures to reduce the environmental impact of the park's large visitor numbers. This includes the use of shuttle systems to reduce traffic, limiting access to sensitive areas, and promoting sustainable travel practices among visitors.

Ways Visitors Can Support Yosemite's Sustainability Initiatives

Visitors play a key role in helping Yosemite remain sustainable. By supporting the park's conservation efforts and making eco-friendly choices during your trip, you can contribute to the protection of this natural wonder.

How You Can Support Yosemite's Sustainability:

- **Reduce Your Carbon Footprint**: Use Yosemite's shuttle system or rent bikes to minimize your use of vehicles in the park. Walking and biking not only reduce emissions but also allow you to experience the park at a slower, more immersive pace.

- **Choose Sustainable Lodging**: Stay in eco-friendly accommodations that prioritize energy efficiency, water conservation, and waste reduction. Some Yosemite lodges, such as **The Ahwahnee** and **Curry Village**, have implemented sustainable practices to reduce their environmental impact.

- **Volunteer**: If you're passionate about conservation, consider participating in Yosemite's **volunteer programs**. Volunteers help with trail maintenance, habitat restoration, and educational programs, contributing to the park's long-term sustainability.

- **Support the Yosemite Conservancy**: The **Yosemite Conservancy** is a nonprofit organization that supports preservation and education efforts in the park. By donating to the conservancy, purchasing items from their stores, or participating in one of their programs, you can help fund projects that protect Yosemite's natural and cultural resources.

- **Follow Park Guidelines**: Always follow the rules and regulations set by the National Park Service, especially regarding food storage, camping, and wildlife interactions. These guidelines are designed to protect the park's ecosystems and ensure a safe and enjoyable experience for all visitors.

Chapter 10

FREQUENTLY ASKED QUESTIONS (FAQS)

Planning a trip to Yosemite National Park can raise a lot of questions, especially if it's your first time visiting. To help you prepare, here are answers to some of the most frequently asked questions about visiting the park, covering everything from reservations and photography to making the most of a short visit.

Do I Need to Make Reservations?

Yes, it's highly recommended to make reservations in advance, especially during the peak season (spring through fall) when Yosemite experiences the highest volume of visitors. Planning ahead will ensure you secure accommodations, permits, and any activities you want to participate in.

Can I Visit Yosemite in One Day?

Yes, it's possible to visit Yosemite in one day, but with so much to see, you'll need to plan carefully to make the most of your short visit. Here are some tips on how to maximize your time in the park and enjoy the best Yosemite has to offer.

How to Make the Most of a Short Visit

Start Early: To make the most of your one-day visit, it's essential to arrive early—ideally by sunrise. Not only will you avoid the crowds, but the soft morning light provides excellent opportunities for photography and sightseeing.

Must-See Spots for a One-Day Trip:

Tunnel View: Begin your day at Tunnel View for a classic introduction to Yosemite Valley. This iconic viewpoint offers stunning vistas of El Capitan, Half Dome, and Bridalveil Fall.

Yosemite Valley Highlights: After Tunnel View, head into Yosemite Valley to explore the valley floor. Stop by Yosemite Falls, El Capitan Meadow, and Sentinel Bridge for photo ops and short walks.

Glacier Point (Optional): If time allows, drive or take a shuttle to Glacier Point for one of the best panoramic views of the park. The drive takes about an hour each way, so it may not fit into a very short visit, but it's worth the effort if you have time.

Bridalveil Fall: This short, easy hike leads to the base of Bridalveil Fall, one of Yosemite's most beautiful waterfalls. It's a quick stop, but the view is well worth it.

El Capitan and Valley View: Spend some time at Valley View, located along Northside Drive, for an impressive view of El Capitan reflected in the Merced River.

Maximize Your Time:

Pack a Picnic: Instead of stopping for a sit-down meal, pack a picnic or grab food from Degnan's Kitchen or Curry Village. Find a scenic spot like Cathedral Beach or El Capitan Meadow to enjoy your lunch while soaking in the views.

Use the Shuttle: To save time and avoid parking hassles, use the free shuttle service in Yosemite Valley. The shuttle runs frequently and stops at most major attractions in the valley.

If You Have Extra Time:

Mist Trail: If you're an active hiker, consider squeezing in a hike on the Mist Trail to Vernal Fall. This popular trail offers close-up views of one of Yosemite's most powerful waterfalls. It's a moderate hike, but the stunning views make it worth the effort.

Evening Farewell:

Sunset at Tunnel View or Glacier Point: End your day with sunset views at Tunnel View or, if time allows head back up to Glacier Point for a memorable finale to your Yosemite visit.

CONCLUSION

Yosemite National Park is not just a destination—it's an experience that connects visitors with nature's most awe-inspiring wonders. From its towering granite cliffs and majestic waterfalls to its quiet meadows and hidden trails, Yosemite offers something for every type of adventurer. Whether you come for a day or stay for a week, the park's natural beauty, rich history, and diverse wildlife will leave a lasting impression.

As you explore the iconic landmarks, immerse yourself in the high country, or discover off-the-beaten-path gems, it's important to remember the role we play in preserving this incredible landscape. Practicing responsible travel, respecting wildlife, and supporting conservation efforts ensures that Yosemite's grandeur will continue to inspire future generations.

In the end, Yosemite is more than just a park—it's a reminder of the power and beauty of the natural world. Whether you're hiking the trails, photographing the vistas, or simply enjoying a peaceful moment by a river, Yosemite's timeless splendor offers a profound sense of connection and renewal. We hope this guide has helped you prepare for your journey and that your time in this remarkable place is filled with unforgettable memories.

Made in the USA
Las Vegas, NV
28 December 2024

15508352R00066